TABLE OF CONTENTS

CHAPTER I KETOSIS FOR WOMEN OVER 50 ------------------3

WHAT IS THE KETO DIET EXACTLY? --------------------------------5

BENEFITS OF FOLLOWING A KETOGENIC DIET ----------------------6

KETOSIS FOR LONGEVITY--10

HOW TO GET INTO KETOSIS --------------------------------------10

CHAPTER II FOODS TO AVOID WHEN ON THE KETO DIET 12

CHAPTER III TIPS FOR SUSTAINING A KETO MEAL PLAN -16

CHAPTER IV BEST EXERCISES FOR WOMEN OVER 50-----27

CHAPTER V TIPS FOR STARTING A WORKOUT ROUTINE AT 50+ --35

CHAPTER VI GREAT WEIGHT LOSS TIPS-------------------39

CHAPTER VII 7-DAY KETO MEAL PLAN --------------------47

CONCLUSION ---99

INTRODUCTION

The ketogenic diet or keto diet is a high fat, low carbohydrate way of eating. It allows for moderate amounts of proteins, natural fats like coconut oil or butter and vegetables.

Women of over 50 can make the switch and start to realize the benefits, however, just like with any diet plan, it can be tricky at first as you try to learn what foods you can and can't eat.

It's any diet that forces the body into a process called ketosis. This is the process where fats are burned for energy instead of using carbohydrates for energy. Doing it correctly, the keto diet asks the dieter to consume high amounts of fats, moderate amounts of protein and very low amounts of carbs.

With a traditional diet, our bodies normally turn carbohydrates into glucose that's sent throughout the body as a source for energy. On the keto diet, we enter ketosis by limiting our carbohydrates, causing our livers to start breaking down fat cells into fatty acids and ketones to be used as energy.

If you're a 50+ woman, who is thinking about giving the keto diet a try or you've already decided but finding it difficult to figure out the list of meals or snacks that are acceptable, then you'll want to read on.

Chapter I
Ketosis for Women Over 50

Many attribute pain and sickness to old age, but getting older does not equate to getting sicker — at least, it doesn't have to. Not only will we explore the connection between aging and health, this book will also take analyze how diet and lifestyle play a big part in ensuring that we live a long and healthy life. Whether you have a loved one in your life that is age 50+ or if you fall within that age category, let's take a look at how ketosis for seniors can help everyone enjoy the golden years.

Part of aging does involve a degree of decline in how we can function, but it doesn't have to be debilitating and isolating. Unfortunately, this is the sad reality for many women and elders in our society. The high-carb, processed diet often prescribed for people of this age group is not helping either.

Rather than seeing getting older as unfortunate, we can support healthier mental and physical health at any age, through a more appropriate diet. And the truth is: there are many advantages of following a ketogenic diet for senior adults.

What Is the Keto Diet Exactly?

The keto diet, shortened from ketogenic, is a particularly low-carb, high-fat diet that's very similar to other low-carb diets, including the Atkins approach. The keto diet radically reduces carbohydrate intake, while substituting the body's main energy sources with fats. This decline in carb usage leads the body to a metabolic state called ketosis.

When this happens, your metabolism starts to burn fat for energy. This process is so amazingly efficient and it results in weight loss, along with other health benefits. The not-so-obvious advantages of eating keto foods are being hungry less often and having a constant amount of energy, which can help keep you sharp and focused during the day.

Ketogenic diets are characterized by a massive decrease in blood sugar and insulin levels. Sugar is the brain's main food, but fortunately, the brain can also be fed with ketones, which are produced from fat in the liver.

Benefits of Following a Ketogenic Diet

Here are some of the ways being in ketosis and eating healthy ketogenic foods can address concerns often faced by seniors today:

Inflammation

For many women, aging includes more pain from injuries that happened at a younger age or joint issues like arthritis. Being in ketosis can help reduce the production of substances called cytokines that promote inflammation, which can help with these types of conditions.

Nutrient Deficiencies

Older adults tend to have higher deficiencies in important nutrients like:

Iron: deficiency can lead to brain fog and fatigue.

Vitamin B12: deficiency can lead to neurological conditions like dementia.

Fats: deficiency can lead to problems with cognition, skin, vision, and vitamin intake levels.

Vitamin D: deficiency causes cognitive impairment in older adults, increases the risk of heart disease, and even contributes to cancer risk.

The high-quality sources of animal protein in the ketogenic diet can easily account for these important nutrients.

Insulin Resistance

Many senior citizens in our society are overweight and dealing with insulin-related conditions like diabetes. This is serious as diabetes can lead to things like vision loss, kidney disease and more.

Bone Health

Osteoporosis, which is the reduction of bone density, causes bones to become fragile and brittle. It is one of the most common conditions seen in older men and women. More calcium through daily intake of milk products, as the USDA recommends, obviously isn't the answer because the countries with the highest rates of osteoporosis tend to have the highest rates of dairy consumption. A much better option is to focus on a keto diet low in toxins, which interferes with absorption and is rich in all micronutrients, rather than overloaded on a specific macronutrient (calcium).

Controlling Blood Sugar

There is a connection between poor blood sugar and brain-related conditions like Alzheimer's disease, Dementia, and Parkinson's Disease. Some factors that might contribute to Alzheimer's disease include:

An excessive intake of carbohydrates, especially from fructose: This is drastically reduced in the ketogenic diet.

A lack of dietary fats and cholesterol: These are abundant and healthy on the ketogenic diet.

Oxidative stress: You are protected against thisduring ketosis.

Using a ketogenic diet to help control blood sugar and improve nutrition can help in the improvement of insulin response and also protects against memory problems that often develop with age.

Importance of Keto for Aging

Keto foods deliver a high amount of nutrition per calorie. This is important because basal metabolic rate (the amount of calories needed daily to survive) is less for seniors, but they still need the same amount of nutrients as younger people.

A person age 50+ will have a much harder time living on junk foods than a teen or 20-something whose body is still resilient. This makes it even more crucial for seniors to eat foods that are health-supporting and disease-fighting. It can literally mean the difference between enjoying the golden years to the fullest or spending them in pain and agony.

Therefore, seniors need to eat more optimal diets by avoiding "empty calories" from sugars or foods rich in anti-nutrients, such as whole grains, and increasing their amount of nutrient-rich fats and proteins.

Additionally, much of the food chosen by older people (or given in a hospital or clinical settings) tends to be heavily processed and very poor in nutrients, such as white breads, pastas, prunes, mashed potatoes, puddings, etc.

It's pretty clear that the high-carb diet so widely pushed by the government is not best for supporting our senior citizens and their long-term health. A diet low in carbohydrates and rich in animal and plant fats is more ideal for promoting better insulin sensitivity, less instances of cognitive decline and overall better health.

Ketosis for Longevity

No matter our age, it's never a bad idea to improve your chances of feeling and functioning well for the rest of your life. It's never too late to start doing better, even though the sooner we start, the better our chances are of avoiding disease. Even for those who have spent many years not treating their bodies as well as they should, ketosis for seniors has the potential to repair some of the damage.

How to Get into Ketosis

The main goal of the keto diet is to get into ketosis, i.e., get your body to start burning fat. How do you do this? First, the most important thing is to restrict carbohydrates to 20 grams per day or less. This requirement satisfies the strict, low-carb keto diet principles. However, dietary fiber (which is technically a carb) should not be limited, since it actually helps you in achieving ketosis. If you aren't sure how much 20 grams of carbs is, you can use published keto diet recipes and meal plans, which are all designed with less than 20 grams of carbs. Thus, no counting is required.

The good news is that just restricting carbs to produce some level of deficiency eventually results in ketosis. To be more satisfied with your keto diet results, you have to go through some additional steps, like regulating your protein intake and increasing your fat intake.

Secondly, your protein intake should be limited to moderate levels because excess protein is converted to glucose in the body, which reduces ketosis. Therefore, about 1.5 grams of protein per kg of body weight per day are enough if you want to maintain a proper diet.

Thirdly, eating enough fat is crucial to staying satisfied. If you add intermittent fasting, ketosis will come even faster. However, unlike hunger, a keto diet is sustainable and can make you feel great. One option if you feel hungry all the time is to add more fat (butter, olive oil, etc.) in your meals.

Chapter II
Foods to Avoid When On the Keto Diet

It is important to note that this diet is a pretty easy one to follow, so don't be discouraged by all the off-limit foods. If you have motivation, it's easy after that. Once you're in, you will realize you're not hungry..

So, if you're over 50 and are interested in trying the keto diet to lose weight, here are advices focusing on what not to eat.

No Ice Cream.

Ice cream – "that's a no," says Dr. Tan. "Learn to cook. Buy whipped cream and whip it yourself."

No Caffeine.

Something that a lot of keto dieters don't realize is that caffeine intake can be harmful if you're in ketosis. Caffeine produces a spike in your glucose. It's a gray area. You can have caffeine, but definitely not all the time. You don't want a continuous spike of sugar.

No Fruit.

You have to focus on cutting out carbs. And yes – that includes fruit. You can't eat fruit because of the sugar. This also includes tomatoes.

No Milk.

A lot of people don't think about cow's milk as having carbs, but it does! Instead, it is best to consume soy, coconut or almond milk as an alternative.

Meat Is Fine, But Limit Processed Meat.

Choose fresh meat over processed meat. The concern is that most processed meat contains sodium nitrite, a chemical preservative linked to increased colon cancer risk.

If everyone just ate meat from the farm, they'd be better off.

Limit Keto Baked Goods.

You have to watch out with those, because they do have sweeteners added that can make you hungry.

Xylitol and sugar alcohols in general – you can spot them because they end in "-ol" – should be avoided. They'll make you hungry, causing you to increase your calorie intake.

Once you start increasing the amount you eat, you're no longer restricting calories, so the ketogenic diet should be treated like a drug. Anything in excess is bad.

Nothing Labeled "Fat-Free."

Shy away from any products labeled as "fat-free," because they likely have starch added. A common product that tricks keto dieters is mayo. Make sure it's real mayo!

Watch Out For Ketchup And Spice Blends.

Ketchup and spices have hidden sugars. Next time you're walking through the spice aisle, take a close look at the ingredients list. You may be surprised to find that one of the first ingredients is sugar!

No Bread, Rice, Potatoes, Soda, Cookies, Candy, Chocolates.

Once again, avoiding carbs is the key. All of these carb-heavy foods and snacks are a no-go when doing the keto diet (or any diet, really!).

Chapter III
Tips for Sustaining a Keto Meal Plan

Below are the best ways to do keto diet. I hope you enjoy it.

Stay In Ketosis By Keeping Your Carbs Very Low and Sticking To It

The number one, most important thing for the keto diet is to keep your net carbs sufficiently low, in order to get into ketosis and stay there.

"Sufficiently low", for most people, means 20-25 g net carbs a day and for some people, that amount might be higher. However, we recommend being strict and sticking to that limit at least until you are fat-adapted (which usually takes around 4 to 6 weeks).

Cheating might be detrimental to your success and might have a number of side effects, including slowing down the adaptation process. So, do your body a service by letting it stay in ketosis.

Get Enough Sleep and Rest

Losing weight also depends on your stress levels — high cortisol levels lead to weight retention or even weight gain.

While stressful life events do happen and you cannot control these, you can ensure that you're getting enough sleep and that you're well-rested.

In order for the body to properly recover every night, most people need a solid 7 to 9 hours of sleep. If you are not getting enough sleep on a regular basis, it will be detrimental not only to your weight loss but also to your overal health.

Use 28-days keto challenge...

The 28-Day Keto Challenge is a detailed and comprehensive plan that will guide you through the first month of your keto diet.

It will provide you with a list of foods that you can and cannot eat, which will make sticking to your new diet much easier.

There are a lot of other information in this guide that will help you stay on track through the first 28 days.

Keep It Simple – Aim For Consistency By Sticking To The Basics

When you first start keto, you'll probably feel confused and overwhelmed by all of the information out there.

Keto doesn't have to be complicated though, and in order to succeed, you need to keep it simple enough to follow on a daily basis. Consistency is key, and keeping it simple will make that much easier.

To be successful, you need to adhere to the following: choose a protein source you like (meat, fish, eggs...), along with your favorite low-carb side (green salad, spinach, cauliflower, avocado, etc...), and add fat as necessary.

Throw in a treat (such as fat bombs) if it'll help you stick with your diet and add some berries from time to time if you like. And that's it.

If You're Stalling, Try Cutting Dairy And Nuts From Your Diet

There is nothing wrong with dairy and nuts per se; they just tend to be very calorically dense and most people do not track them properly. Additionally, they might cause digestive issues for some people and be slightly inflammatory, leading to bloating and water retention.

If you're struggling, try to limit or stop eating dairy and nuts for 2-3 weeks to see if that makes a difference, and then reintroduce them slowly by observing how your body reacts to these foods.

Track Your Macros and Calories

Tracking your macros is essential when doing keto, especially when you're starting out.

You'll soon notice that carbs are everywhere. In order to avoid consuming too many carbs, it's essential to plan, measure and track everything that you're eating.

Additionally, to lose weight, you'd still need to create a caloric deficit, even on keto (yeah, keto isn't magic... although we wish it were).

To do that, you first need to figure out what your maintenance calories are, i.e., the number of calories you need to eat in order to maintain your weight.

Afterward, you need to subtract 10% to 25% from that number. Larger deficits (20% to 25%) will normally lead to a more rapid weight loss but might be difficult to sustain, as they are more stressful for your body and you'll experience more hunger.

Dieting with a lower deficit (around 15% to 20%) will lead to a slower weight loss, but it is psychologically and physically more forgiving. Also, the weight you lose slowly is usually easier to keep off.

Understand That It's Necesssary To Change Your Lifestyle In Order To Achieve Long-term Weight Loss

Weight losss can be long-term only if you adapt healthy habits and change your lifestyle.

If you just do keto for a couple of months and then go back to the things that made you gain weight in the first place, you risk regaining the weight and then some more.

Yo-yo dieting is something a lot of people have gone through, and it is both extremely discouraging and very taxing, both mentally and physically.

In order for your weight losss to stick, you need to re-evaluate your relationship with food and eventually with physical activity too, if you're very sedentary.

Staying keto for the long-term (or for life) is a path many people choose because of the many health benefits that the keto diet has. But it's not an absolute necessity.

Others have chosen a more liberal approach to their diet by staying low-carb, Paleo or primal. Whatever your choice is, make sure to stay active while eating nutrient-dense, whole foods that are not carb-heavy.

Skip meals

Thinking of breakfast as the most important meal of the day could be easily changed when on this diet. If you aren't starved when you wake up, you can skip breakfast, grab a ⯑uick keto shake or have a cup of coffee alone. A reduced appetite is a common feature of the diet, so skipping a meal isn't a problem. However, if you are hungry when you wake up but are short on time, a keto breakfast can be tasty, filling, and ⯑uick to prepare.

Move More

While not strictly keto-related, moving aroud more is an excellent strategy to increase the calories you're burning in a day.

This doesn't necessarily mean working out; in fact, if you think about it, working out is just a tiny portion of your day and week.

You can try adding more "non-exercise" activities to your days, such as walking, working in your garden (or any other hobby that has a physical element to it), cleaning, taking the stairs more often, and so on.

If you have an office job, you should try getting up from your desk and moving around at least every hour or so.

A strategy you can try out as well is to do a ⯑uick exercise each time something specific happens.

For example: do 15 squats each time you go to the toilet, do a couple of push-ups after waking up or get up and move while talking on your mobile phone.

There are many different things you can try out but one thing is certain — by moving more, you'll help your body burn more energy.

Track Your Progress In A Few Different Ways

Your progress might not always show on the scale, even if you look and feel different. Why is that, you might wonder?

When losing weight, our bodies often retain water, and releases it only after a couple of days or weeks.

Alternatively, if you're also actively exercising, and especially if you're doing resistance training, you might be gaining muscle mass while actually losing fat (yes, it's possible).

Use a few different ways to track your progress, and don't get discouraged if the scale doesn't seem to move. Here are some ideas:

Body measures (for example, measure your neck, waist, hip, thighs)

Photos (if you don't take "before" photos at the beginning of your journey, you might regret it later)

The size of your clothes and how they fit.

Go For Maintenance Calories Every Once In A While

Being in a deficit with calories for a long period of time is stressful for your body and your metabolism will adjust with time. To counteract that and to give yourself a small break from dieting, you can adjust your calories back to maintenance level every once in a while.

For example: for every 4 weeks of deficit, you can do 1 week of maintenance calories. This will bring your hormones back to normal levels and will help with weight loss in the long run.

Prepare your own meals

Delicious meals for lunch or dinner can be easily prepared by including meat or fish with a salad, for example. A vegetarian keto diet is also an option—e.g., vegetables cooked with melted butter, cheese or a rich sauce.

Load up on keto vegetables

The keto vegetables include celery, spinach, asparagus, avocado, zucchini, cauliflower, cucumber, cabbage, broccoli, kale and brussels sprouts. As you may notice, most of them are green and they grow above ground. This is a quick way to tell which vegetable has too many carbs.

Eat Less Often and Try Intermittent Fasting

Snacking, especially if you do it out of boredom or stress, can be detrimental to your weight loss.

Try to stick to 2 or 3 big meals a day and keep snacking to a minimum. Eating less often will help you keep your insulin lower and will also feel more satisfying.

If you are actually hungry or need to go for a long time without a real meal (while on the road, for example), you can have the occasional snack, of course. What is important is to break the habit of eating when you're bored, sad or stressed, and to try to have fewer but larger meals.

Intermittent fasting has many health benefits beyond just weight loss and combining keto diet with fasting can be an optimal way to lose your unwanted body fat.

Accept That Mistakes Happen, Forgive Yourself and Move On

You have cheated and now feel bloated and miserable. That sucks but it has happened to everyone.

Mistakes do and will happen and in such cases, the best thing you can do is just to forgive yourself and move on.

Go back to keto with your next meal and just make sure to not turn your cheat meal into a cheat weekend or a cheat month.

Consistency is key. Mistakes will not erase your progress if you don't let them do that. Keep calm and keto on.

Keep An Eye On Your Electrolytes

Electrolytes are super important while on keto because they get flushed from your system at a higher rate.

To prevent cravings, headaches, cramps, excessive hunger and water retention, you need to make sure that you're getting in enough sodium, magnesium, and potassium.

It's best to get potassium from food, but you'll likely need to supplement some sodium (i.e. salt) and magnesium to make sure everything is running smoothly.

Accept The Fact That Weight Loss Takes Time, Even With Keto

Keto is one of the best diets for weight loss out there, but it will still take time to reach your ideal goal weight.

You need to be patient and consistent in order to get results – gaining the weight didn't happen overnight, right? Losing it is no different.

Your body doesn't like change – it likes stability and predictability. It cannot differentiate between a voluntary weight loss and a possible famine.

If you lose weight very quickly, you're much more likely to gain it back once you stop dieting than if you rely on a slow and steady progress that doesn't put an enormous amount of stress on your body.

Chapter IV
Best Exercises for Women Over 50

Age really is just a number. You might be 55, but look 40 and feel 35. Or, you might be 50, but look and feel 65. It all has to do with how well you care for your body and what you do to stay active.

When it comes to exercise, many people assume if they weren't active during their 20s, 30s or 40s, there's no point in getting started in their 50s or even later. Fortunately, that's just not true. It's never too late to start an exercise program. Starting a workout routine can help reverse some of the problems caused by inactivity and can make you feel great about yourself overall.

Let's take a closer look at the benefits of exercise for women over the age of 50 and at some of the different types of exercises that will help you feel your best.

Muscles in Motion

Set to music from the 1950s and '60s, Muscles in Motion helps you tighten and tone your upper and lower body, with a particular focus on the abdominal muscles. The group class uses hand weights, resistance bands and exercise balls to build strength.

How to Tighten Your Butt with Resistance Bands

Just like lifting a heavier weight, adding resistance to a lower body exercise makes it more intense. If you want a truly effective butt workout, add resistance bands to your donkey kicks and leg lifts. You'll be seeing results in no time.

Lose Weight with the Walk Fast/Slow Plan

This plan will ease you into running. It's a step-by-step guide that is perfect for anyone who is new to running, or people getting back into it after an injury or extended absence. For many women, walking, jogging or running is all the cardio they need to stay healthy.

Plank Pose

The plank not only helps to strengthen and tone your core muscles — aka, your abdominal and lower back muscles — it can improve your balance too. Planks can also help straighten your posture, which is a plus if you sit in a chair for much of the day.

There are several ways to do a plank. For a high plank, get into a position as if you are at the top of a push-up, with your arms and legs straight.

Another option is a low plank, which can be easier to do if you're a beginner. Instead of supporting yourself on your hands, bend your arms at the elbow and support your weight on your forearms.

No matter which version you choose, keep your back completely straight and your head up. Your entire body should form a straight line parallel to the ground.

On-The-Mat Six Pack Workout

This is a basic mat workout you can do anywhere and anytime. You'll notice your abs burning after the first few moves. The trick to getting visible results is to keep your core engaged throughout the workout. Focus on keeping proper form and contracting the abdominal muscles.

6-Minute Arm Toning Workout

This dumbbell arm workout will teach you all the basic lifting exercises you need to tone your arms. It will target your biceps, triceps, shoulders, and a little bit of your upper back. Beginners can start with a single round and slowly work their way up from there.

Squats With A Chair

Another weight-burning exercise that's easy to do at home is squats with a chair. During this exercise, you squat over a chair as if you were about to sit down, but don't make contact with the seat. Instead, you stand back up and repeat the process multiple times.

Squats not only help tone your lower body, but they can also help improve balance. When you get started, you might find it's easiest to perform the exercise with your hands and arms extended out in front of you.

Chest Fly

Women tend to have very weak and underdeveloped chest muscles. The chest fly is a weightlifting exercise that helps strengthen those muscles.

To do the exercise, you'll need a pair of hand weights. Lie on the floor or a mat, flat on your back, with your knees bent and your feet flat on the ground. Take one weight in each hand and raise your arms over your chest.

Slowly, open your arms out to the side, lowering your arms and wrists toward the floor — but don't actually touch the ground. Keep a slight bend in your elbows, so you don't lock out your arms. Raise your arms back up and repeat.

Before Breakfast Mini Morning Workout

A morning workout is more energizing than a cup of coffee. Not to mention cheaper too! This 6-minute workout combines yoga with some basic bodyweight moves to wake you gently. It'll help you stretch, get your blood flowing, and even rev up your mind.

S.O.S.

If you are particularly concerned about the risk of osteoporosis or are concerned about bone loss, S.O.S. is the fitness class for you. It focuses on resistance exercises that help improve bone health and muscle mass.

SilverSneakers Classic

SilverSneakers exercise programs are available free of charge to people on Medicare. The classic program focuses on strength training as well as aerobic activities. Designed for all fitness levels, there are modifications available for people who need additional support or assistance.

Summer Slim Down Workout for Beginners

It's cardio without the treadmill. However, if you push through this workout at a quick pace, you'll burn more calories than you would have running! Squats, walking lunges, hip twists, toe touches, and planks, all activate large muscle groups that help you burn tons of calories. Do this workout 2 to 3 times per week to up your calorie burn.

30-Minute Upper Body Cardio Workout

This 30-minute routine is a complete workout. If you do this, you don't have to do anything else for the day, other than a quick warm-up and cool-down. This workout is more advanced than some of the others on this list, so it's ideal for women who are already fit.

3 Moves to Toned Inner Thighs

This quick 3-move workout is a combination of cardio and lower body strength training. While the moves will challenge your muscles, therefore making them grow stronger, the kicking and stepping also raises your heart rate. You'll be burning calories even while you build muscle.

10-Minute Beginner's Yoga Workout for Balance

One mistake women in their 50s often make is assuming they'll never be able to complete a workout if they don't get through it their first time. The point of this yoga workout is to slowly improve your balance and flexibility. You may struggle with the poses at first! Be persistent and you'll love the results.

Chapter V
Tips For Starting A Workout Routine At 50+

It's never too late to start exercising. Maybe it hasn't been a priority of yours, but eventually, a lack of movement will catch up with you. Regular activity is necessary to stay healthy and prevent common age-related maladies like heart disease, high blood pressure, obesity, and diabetes. It also encourages healthy muscles, joints, and bones.

We get it; if you've never exercised before, it can be hard to start. But studies have shown that just starting a workout routine later in life has a wide range of benefits, like boosting heart health. Here's how you can begin introducing regular exercise into your life after 50.

Find your motivation.

First things first; why do you want to start working out? Maybe your doctor prescribed more activity, you're hoping to trim down a bit or you just want more energy to keep up with your grandkids. Finding your reason for being more active will help to keep you focused on it as a goal. Eventually, it will become a part of your lifestyle, and after noticing how good staying active makes you feel, it will be much easier to do.

Keep it regular.

It's called a routine for a reason. To see any benefit from exercise for the 50+ crowd, doctors recommend at least 30 minutes of moderate to vigorous aerobic activity at least two days each week, such as brisk walking and muscle strengthening exercises. Tempted to skip workouts? Try finding a way to hold yourself accountable, whether that means meeting a friend for weekly walks, pre-registering for group classes (meaning you're losing money if you don't go) or scheduling sessions with your gym's personal trainer.

Start slowly.

The truth is, your body just can't recover as quickly as you age, so if you are trying to start a workout routine for the first time, focus on low-intensity exercises that won't leave you overly sore (or worse, injured). Try some at-home strength workouts to get going, then slowly work up to light weightlifting at the gym, yoga or fitness classes, or more high-intensity training. Try to leave at least 48 hours between training the same muscle group to allow recovery time. And most importantly, listen to your body. If something doesn't feel right, don't overdo it.

Try out a variety ofactivities.

Experiment a little with different types of workouts and find what feels right for you. Join a gym and try out the different fitness classes they have to offer. Eventually, you may find one that sticks. Or ditch the gym and go for a bike ride, take a hike, do a drop-in Zumba class or swim some laps at the local pool. Experts say it's good to focus on a combination of strength training, cardiovascular training and balance training, so trying out different types of exercise will benefit you overall.

You don't have to go to the gym to workout.

Plenty of activities can get you moving and keep you healthy. Gardening, walking the dog, playing with your grandkids or going on a hike or bike ride are all great ways to burn some calories. All these can be peppered into your day naturally and enjoyably. Exercise doesn't have to be a chore!

Incorporate some strength-training and flexibility exercises.

While light, daily activity and getting 10,000 steps a day is extremely beneficial to your health, it's also essential to work-in strength, balance, and flexibility training to your exercise routine. Without some kind of strength-building exercises, your muscles will start to atrophy and lose mass as you get older, increasing your risk of injury. Try light weight-lifting or yoga for balance and flexibility and make sure to stretch after every workout!

Chapter VI
Great Weight Loss Tips

Here are some great weight loss tips to help you reach your fitness and body composition goals. All the weight loss tips in the world won't do a bit of good if nobody can remember to follow them. You don't even have to follow all of these tips. For starters just pick one and when that becomes a habit, try the next weight loss tip that strikes your fancy.

The most important weight loss idea has to do with the Law of Thermodynamics. This law means that in order to lose weight, you need to spend more energy than you take in. In order to gain weight, you need to take more energy in than you put out. So, losing weight is simple; eat less food while moving more often! The weight loss tips below are just ways to take advantage and make more efficient use of this unavoidable law of nature.

Grains And Colorful Food

Whole grains and some colorful produce are rich in phytonutrients and complex carbohydrate, yet low in calories and almost zero fat. Good sources of vitamin A, C, and K, fiber, potassium and folate are vegetables and fruits. Darker color tones will provide wealthier health benefits.

The phytonutrients in whole grains are also found to help prevent diabetes, heart disease and fight against cancer. Whole grains require longer digestion, thus preventing hunger much longer. The recommended choice is foods made of 100% whole grains with diverse types of carbohydrates, containing all the required minerals and vitamins.

Keep A Food Log.

Write down everything you eat for 3 days (every single calorie!) then add up the calories and divide by 3 to get an average. Now that you know how many calories you are taking in, you can plan out how much you need to reduce per day in order to reach your goals.

Cutting Out Sugar

Cutting out sugary sodas and other sugary drinks. A typical regular can of soda has about 140-170 calories. Two of those per day equals 280-340 calories a day or about ¾ lb weight loss per week if you were maintaining your weight before that change. What do you drink instead? Cold water!!! Not only is water healthy, one ounce of cold water will burn one calorie when your body heat is up. So, drinking the recommended 64-96 oz. of water per day could equal up to 96 extra calories burned (depending on how much cold water you drank before).

It doesn't have to be sugary drinks. It could be cutting out desserts, or limiting them to once or twice a week from every day. Try replacing one unhealthy snack per day with a healthier one. You pick one that you can stick to (but start drinking more water anyway).

Daily Journal

Penning down your food consumption every day could be the pathway to keep you reminded of your goal. A record of your daily activities, food intake and emotional sentiments may help you to discover the cause of your overeating or weight gain. It may sound ridiculous but when you know that you need to write down what you eat, even the tastiest food may turn your appetite off. According to the National Weight Control Registry, most dieters practice journalling before succeeding in their plan.

Make a habit of submitting your food journal at least once a day. You can also do it few times a day if you tend to forget what you eat. Then your journal will be the reference of your food intake for further analysis and feedback.

Six Meals Daily

Frequent, small portion of healthy meals will boost metabolism as food has some thermal effect. The recommended figure is six meals for men while five for women. This is never too much and it is time you put this into practice. Eating often will involve calorie burning during food absorption and breakdown.

The positive effect could be 10 times better when you dwell on fre uent eating. In fact, you will be more energetic and less hungry. However the last meal should be at least an hour before you sleep. Unlike other diet plans, this way of eating will not cause deprivation. You may have difficulties when dealing with consistent eating but the effect could turn out reat.

Do not leave your stomach empty for too long because hunger can make you prone to more food binging. Proper meals three times per day is good to cope with your hunger.

Importance Of Protein

According to the Journal of Nutrition published by University of Illinois, having more protein in the food during weight loss can help to get rid of body fat and retain the muscle mass. The presence of L-leucine, an amino acid, will provide spare muscles during weight loss, so only the fat are eliminated. Sustaining your muscles during your diet period can boost the calorie burning activity. Excess protein may cause calcium leaching from your bones and damage to your kidneys, so go moderately with the amount.

You should also try getting lean protein from beans, meat, fish and low-fat dairy products.

Reduce Stress.

Stress causes our body to release cortisol, which is a hormone that helps us deal physiologically with stress. Simply put, the adaptations our body does in response to stress are contrary to weight loss. The release of cortisol promotes fat storage and suppresses the manufacture of other hormones that promote building of lean muscle mass. Try yoga, try meditation, try a hobby or punching a heavy bag. Just do what works for you to lower stress.

Watch Your Calories Intake

Determine how many calories you need to maintain your current weight, and how many you need to reduce per day to meet your weight loss goals.

Determine your basal metabolic rate. This is how many calories your body burns just to maintain minimal life-support functions and is about 75% of all the calories you burn.

Now, to determine how many calories you need each day to maintain your current weight, multiply the base metabolic rate by a "lifestyle factor" based on how active you are. A note on the formula: it is just a rough estimate. Females will need a few less calories (perhaps 200) than this formula indicates. Males might need 100 more. As you age, you will require fewer calories as well to maintain weight. So, use the formula to get you started, then adjust your daily caloric needs based on your results.

For sedentary people (office workers, people who mostly sit or drive all day), use 1.4. For moderately active people (people on their feet all day like wait staff, service industry, moderate exercise), use 1.6. For very active people (jobs with lots of physical labor, movers, etc., athletes), use 1.8. If you think you are in between two of the examples, then you can split the difference.

Let's plug some numbers in: Weight 195 pounds, office worker. 195X10 = 1950 calorie basal metabolic rate. 1950 X 1.4 = 2730. This is roughly how many calories they need to consume to stay at 195 pounds. It's not an exact science, but should be very close and is a great starting point.

Now you can set your weight loss goals based on how many pounds you want to lose and in what time-frame. The maximum sustainable healthy weight loss level is about 2 pounds per week. In order to lose 2 pounds per week, you need to decrease your energy intake, and/or increase your energy output by 1000 calories per day. A 500 calorie per day reduction will result in a loss of approximately one pound per week.

So, losing 40 pounds will take 20 weeks, or about 5 months at 2lbs per week if you decrease your daily intake by 500 calories per day as well as increase your energy expenditure by an average of 500 calories per day. From our example above, to lose 2 lbs per week, they would either need to eat 1730 calories per day (2730-1000) or 2230 calories with about 500 calories worth of exercise averaged out over each day.

Pamper Yourself

Everybody loves reward, so you can certainly pamper yourself with something you like when you achieve any small goals. Rewarding yourself will enhance your confidence and a higher self-esteem will prevent you from food binging. However, one important note - the reward should not be in the form of food. Shopping, spa, or movies are way better.

Move more!

This doesn't mean you have to start some grueling exercise program. In the beginning, look for ways to move a little more than normal. Take the stairs instead of the elevator. Walk to the store down the street or the park instead of driving and when you do start an exercise program, start slow and easy. No more than 3 days per week in the beginning. Twenty minutes of walking 3 times per week is a great start. Or, 3 shorts workouts at the gym or at home per week. This will start to increase your caloric expenditure so you don't have to cut quite so many calories out of your diet and still lose weight.

Select Healthy Meals

You can try out a variety of seasonings, the best cooking method or different vegetables to decide what is best for you before you start your diet plan. A good plan will help to avoid messy decisions and you will have an advanced supply of food to kick off towards your goal. Shopping once a week is rather significant, as running out of good food will have you eating inappropriately. Containers such as jugs, bottles and a cooler will be handy to store your food within reach.

Do not allow hunger to wait. Tiny, healthy snacks are better than an empty stomach. A good breakfast can help to keep your hunger under control. Besides, water is also great to help reduce your food portions.

Chapter VII
7-Day Keto Meal Plan

Day 1

--Breakfast--

Ham & Cheese Breakfast Roll-Ups

Prep Time: 0 hours 20 mins
Total Time: 0 hours 20 mins
Servingss: 2

Ingredients

4 large eggs
¼ c. milk
2 tbsp. Chopped chives
kosher salt
Freshly ground black pepper
1 tbsp. butter
1 c. shredded cheddar, divided
4 slices ham

Instructions

In a medium bowl, whisk together eggs, milk, and chives. Season with salt and pepper.

In a medium skillet over medium heat, melt butter. Pour half of the egg mixture into the skillet, moving to create a thin layer that covers the entire pan.

Cook for 2 minutes. Add ½ cup cheddar and cover for 2 minutes more, until the cheese is melty. Remove onto plate, place 2 slices of ham, and roll tightly. Repeat with remaining ingredients and serve.

--Lunch--

Cinnamon Pork Chops & Mock Apples

Hearty, healthy, and delicious, cinnamon pork chops with chayote mock apples make a fantastic family dinner or meal prep for the work week!

Prep Time: 5 minutes
Cook Time: 40 minutes
Total Time: 45 minutes

Ingredients

2 tbsp ghee
½ tsp sea salt
4 pork chops boneless
2 chayote chopped to ½ -inch chunks
2 tbsp monkfruit sweetener or low carb sweetener of choice
1 tsp cinnamon
1/8 tsp nutmeg
1 tbsp apple cider vinegar

Instructions

Melt ghee in a large skillet over medium heat, add pork chops and cook for 5 minutes.

Flip the pork chops and add chayote and sprinkle sweetener, cinnamon, nutmeg, and apple cider vinegar over the top. Cook for an additional 4-5 minutes, or until the pork chops reach the appropriate temperature (145 F for medium rare, 160 for medium).

Remove the pork chops and place in a meal prep container if preparing meals for the week. If not, keep pork chops warm until ready to serve.

Bring the chayote mixture to a boil for several minutes. Reduce heat to low medium and simmer with cover, stirring occasionally, for 30 to 40 minutes. When done, the chayote will be fork tender and similar in texture to baked apple.

Divide the chayote mock apples between four meal prep containers or serve immediately alongside the warm pork chops.

Recipe Notes

2g net carbohydrates per serving, which gives you room for a couple more things if you'd like to add that to your meal prep container or tailor things to your personal macros.

Nutrition Info

Net Carbs: 4.85g
Protein: 35.43g
Fat: 30.22g
Calories: 455kcal

--Dinner--

Keto Instant Pot Crack Chicken Recipe

Prep time: 5 mins
Cook time: 20 mins
Total time: 25 mins
8 servings

Ingredients

2 slices bacon, chopped
2 lbs (910 g) boneless, skinless chicken breasts
2 (8 oz/227 g) blocks cream cheese
½ cup (120 ml) water
2 tablespoons apple cider vinegar
1 tablespoon dried chives
1½ teaspoons garlic powder
1½ teaspoons onion powder
1 teaspoon crushed red pepper flakes
1 teaspoon dried dill
¼ teaspoon salt
¼ teaspoon black pepper
½ cup (2 oz/57 g) shredded cheddar
1 scallion, green and white parts, thinly sliced

Instructions

Turn pressure cooker on, press "Sauté" and wait for 2 minutes for the pot to heat up. Add the chopped bacon and cook until crispy. Transfer to a plate and set aside. Press "Cancel" to stop sautéing.

Add the chicken, cream cheese, water, vinegar, chives, garlic powder, onion powder, crushed red pepper flakes, dill, salt, and black pepper to the pot. Turn the pot on Manual, High Pressure for 15 minutes and then do a quick release.

Use tongs to transfer the chicken to a large plate, shred it with 2 forks and return it to the pot.

Stir in the cheddar cheese.

Top with the crispy bacon and scallion, and serve.

Nutrition Info

Calories: 437 Fat: 27.6 Potassium: 390 Net Carbs: 4.3 Carbohydrates: 4.5 Sodium: 420 Fiber: .2 Protein: 41.2

Day 2

Keto Fat Bombs

These fat bombs are your best friends. Don't let the name scare you—these little balls are the perfect way to curb your hunger.

Servingss: 8
Prep Time: 0 hours 5 mins
Total Time: 0 hours 25 mins

Ingredients

8 oz. cream cheese, softened to room temperature
½ c. keto-friendly peanut butter
¼ c. coconut oil, plus 2 tbsp.
½ tsp. kosher salt
1 c. keto-friendly dark chocolate chips (such as Lily's)

Instructions

Line a small baking sheet with parchment paper. In a medium bowl, combine cream cheese, peanut butter, ¼ c coconut oil, and salt. Using a hand mixer, beat mixture until fully combined, about 2 minutes. Place bowl in the freezer to firm up slightly, 10 to 15 minutes.

When peanut butter mixture has hardened, use a small cookie scoop or spoon to create golf ball sized balls. Place in the refrigerator to harden, 5 minutes.

Meanwhile, make chocolate drizzle: combine chocolate chips and remaining coconut oil in a microwave safe bowl and microwave in 30 second intervals until fully melted. Drizzle over peanut butter balls and place back in the refrigerator to harden, 5 minutes. Serve.

To store, keep covered in refrigerator.

--Lunch--

Sesame Salmon w. Baby Bok Choy & Mushrooms

Ingredients

Main Dish

> 4 each 4-6 oz. salmon fillet
> 2 each portobello mushroom caps (or 8 oz. baby bella mushrooms)
> 4 each baby bok choy
> 1 tbsp toasted sesame seeds
> 1 ea green onion

Marinade

> 1 tbsp olive oil
> 1 tsp sesame oil
> 1 tbsp Coconut Aminos
> ½ inch Ginger grated (approx. 1 tsp.)
> ½ lemon juice
> ½ tsp Salt
> ½ tsp black pepper

Instructions

Whisk together all of your marinade ingredients.

Drizzle half of the marinade on the salmon and turn to coat. Cover and refrigerate the salmon while it marinates for one hour.

Preheat oven to 400.

Prepare vegetables: Trim the rough ends from the bok choy and cut into halves. Slice the mushrooms into ½ inch pieces.

Drizzle the remaining marinade over the vegetables and lay on a lined baking sheet.

Place salmon, skin side down, on a lined baking sheet as well. Bake until salmon is cooked through, about 20 minutes.

Top with sliced green onions and sesame seeds.

--Dinner--

Crab Stuffed Mushrooms With Cream Cheese

An easy recipe for crab stuffed mushrooms with cream cheese. Low carb, keto, and gluten free.

Prep Time: 15 minutes
Cook Time: 30 minutes
Servings: 4 servings
Calories: 160 kcal

Ingredients

20 ounces cremini (baby bella) mushrooms (20-25 individual mushrooms)
2 tablespoons finely grated parmesan cheese
1 tablespoon chopped fresh parsley
salt

Filling:

4 ounces cream cheese softened to room temperature
4 ounces crab meat finely chopped
5 cloves garlic minced
1 teaspoon dried oregano
½ teaspoon paprika
½ teaspoon black pepper
¼ teaspoon salt

Instructions

Preheat the oven to 400 F. Prepare a baking sheet lined with parchment paper.

Snap stems from mushrooms. Discard the stems and place the mushroom caps on the baking sheet 1 inch apart from each other. Season the mushroom caps with salt.

In a large mixing bowl, combine all filling ingredients and stir until well-mixed without any lumps of cream cheese. Stuff the mushroom caps with the mixture. Evenly sprinkle parmesan cheese on top of the stuffed mushrooms.

Bake at 400 F until the mushrooms are very tender and the stuffing is nicely browned on top, about 30 minutes. Top with parsley and serve while hot.

Nutrition Info

This recipe serving is 5 g net carbs per serving (5-6 stuffed mushrooms).

Calories: 160
Total Carb: 5.5g 2%
Dietary Fiber: 0.5g 1%
Sugars: 0g
Protein: 9g

Day 3

--Breakfast--

Brussels Sprouts Hash

Servingss: 4
Prep Time: 0 hours 10 mins
Total Time: 0 hours 40 mins

Ingredients

6 slices bacon, cut into 1" pieces
½ onion, chopped
1 lb. brussel sprouts, trimmed and quartered
kosher salt
Freshly ground black pepper
¼ tsp. red pepper flakes
3 tbsp. water
2 garlic cloves, minced
4 large eggs

Instructions

In a large skillet over medium heat, fry bacon until crispy. Turn off heat and transfer bacon to a paper towel-lined plate. Keep most of bacon fat in skillet, removing any black pieces from the bacon.

Turn heat back to medium and add onion and brussel sprouts to the skillet. Cook, stirring occasionally, until the vegetables begin to soften and turn golden. Season with salt, pepper, and red pepper flakes.

Add 2 tablespoons of water and cover the skillet. Cook until the brussel sprouts are tender and the water has evaporated, about 5 minutes. (If all the water evaporates before the brussel sprouts are tender, add more water to the skillet and cover for a couple of minutes more.) Add garlic to skillet and cook until fragrant, 1 minute.

Using a wooden spoon, make four holes in the hash to reveal bottom of skillet. Crack an egg into each hole and season each egg with salt and pepper. Replace lid and cook until eggs are cooked to your liking, about 5 minutes for a just runny egg. Sprinkle cooked bacon bits over the entire skillet. Serve warm.

--Lunch--

Caprese Tuna Salad Stuffed Tomatoes

Prep Time: 10 minutes
Servings: Serves 1

Ingredients

1 medium tomato
1 (5oz) can tuna, very well drained
2 tsp balsamic vinegar
1 TBSP chopped mozzarella {¼ oz.}
1 TBSP chopped fresh basil
1 TBSP chopped green onion

Instructions

Cut the top ¼ inch off the tomato. Use a spoon to scoop out the insides of the tomato. Set aside while you make the tuna salad.

Stir together the drained tuna, balsamic vinegar, mozzarella, basil, and green onion. Put the tuna salad in the hollowed out tomato, and enjoy!

Note: I prefer using fresh mozzarella but any mozzarella is good in here.

Nutrition Info

Calories per serving: 196
Fat per serving: 4.9g

--Dinner--

Keto Chicken Enchilada Bowl

This Keto Chicken Enchilada Bowl is a low carb twist on a Mexican favorite! It's so easy to make, totally filling and ridiculously yummy!

Prep Time: 20 minutes
Cook Time: 30 minutes
Total Time: 50 minutes
Servings: 4

Ingredients

2 tablespoons coconut oil (for searing chicken)
1 pound of boneless, skinless chicken thighs
¾ cup red enchilada sauce (recipe from Low Carb Maven)
¼ cup water
¼ cup chopped onion
4 oz can diced green chiles

Toppings (feel free to customize)

1 whole avocado, diced
1 cup shredded cheese (I used mild cheddar)
¼ cup chopped pickled jalapenos
½ cup sour cream
1 roma tomato, chopped

Optional: serve over plain cauliflower rice (or mexican cauliflower rice) for a more complete meal!

Instructions

In a pot or dutch oven over medium heat, melt the coconut oil. Once hot, sear chicken thighs until lightly brown.

Pour in enchilada sauce and water then add onion and green chillies. Reduce heat to a simmer and cover. Cook chicken for 17-25 minutes or until chicken is tender and fully cooked through to at least 165 degrees internal temperature.

Careully remove the chicken and place onto a work surface. Chop or shred chicken (your preference), then add it back into the pot. Let the chicken simmer uncovered for an additional 10 minutes to absorb flavor and allow the sauce to reduce a little.

To serve, top with avocado, cheese, jalapeno, sour cream, tomato, and any other desired toppings. Feel free to customize these to your preference. Serve alone or over cauliflower rice if desired just be sure to update your personal nutrition info as needed.

Nutrition Info

Calories: 568 Calories

Total Carbs: 10.41g
Fiber: 4.27g
Net Carbs: 6.14g
Protein: 38.38g
Fat: 40.21g

Day 4

Curry Tofu Scramble with Avocado

This tofu scramble is a fabulous low-carb, veggie lover approach to begin the morning. It has a lot of supplements and sufficient calories to give you vitality for the day ahead.

Prep Time: 5 minutes
Total Time: 20 minutes
Cook Time: 13 minutes
Servings: 3

Ingredients:

1 tbsp coconut oil
2 tbsp olive oil
300 g tofu (extra firm)
1 tsp turmeric
1 tbsp nutritional yeast
1 tbsp curry powder
½ cup zucchini (chopped)
1 cup mushrooms (chopped)
1 tomato (chopped)
cilantro (optional)(to garnish)
300-gram avocado

Instructions:

The initial step is to dry the tofu so it ingests the flavor.

Cut the tofu into 1 inch long strips, spread out the strips on a paper towel.

Put another paper towel to finish everything and after that, a slashing board.

Place something substantial over this, for example, a few books.

Abandon it to sit for around 15 minutes.

Add the coconut oil to the dish and disintegrate the tofu into the skillet with your hands.

Cook for around 5 minutes, mixing every now and again.

Include the turmeric, nourishing yeast and curry powder and 1 tbsp of the olive oil,

Blend and cook for a further 4 minutes.

Add whatever remains of the olive oil, zucchini, mushroom and tomato and sear for a further 4 minutes blending much of the time.

Serve with 1 little medium size avocado (roughly 100g) cut.

Recipe Notes:

This meal can be refrigerated for a few days.

Nutrition Info

Calories: 381

Fats: 32g
Protein: 11g
Net Carbs: 8g

--Lunch--

Loaded Chicken Salad

A delicious salad filled with plenty of vegetables and delicious grilled meat!

Prep Time: 10 minutes
Cook Time: 8 minutes
Total Time: 18 minutes
Total Carbs: 12.86g

Ingredients

1 boneless chicken breast (about 300g, with or without skin)
1 tbsp extra virgin olive oil
¼ tsp Himalayan salt
¼ tsp black pepper
1 avocado
100 g mozzarella balls
1 large tomato (any colour)
1 har artichoke hearts (my jar was 170g)
½ red onion
5 asparagus
20 leaves basil
4 cups baby spinach (200g used)

Dressing

2 tbsp extra virgin olive oil
1 1/2 tbsp balsamic vinegar
1 tsp dijon mustard
1 clove garlic
pinch Himalayan salt
pinch black pepper

Instructions

Peel and dice the avocado. Slice the red onion. Dice the tomato. Pile the basil leaves together, roll them up and slice. Cut the stems off the asparagus and slice in half. Mince the garlic.

Slice the chicken breast in half lengthwise. Sprinkle the 1/4 tsp of salt and pepper on each sides. Heat the 1 tbsp of olive oil in a cast iron skillet and place the chicken breasts in. Fry on each side, about 3 minutes each side until they have a nice golden brown colour and cooked through. Add the asparagus beside the chicken breasts and cook for a few minutes until soft and grilled. Take out the chicken and slice.

In a small bowl, combine the minced garlic, olive oil, balsamic vinegar, dijon, and salt & peper.

Add the baby spinach to a large bowl or plate. Cover with the grilled chicken, avocado, mozzarella, tomatoes, artichoke, red onions, asparagus and basil leaves. Pour the dressing over and enjoy!

Notes

You can add 1 tbsp of honey to the salad dressing if you don't mind the extra carbs or want a sweeter dressing.

Nutrition Info

Calories: 430
Calories from Fat: 264

Total Fat: 29.36g 45%
Saturated: Fat 6.57g 33%
Total Carbohydrates: 12.86g 4%
Dietary Fiber: 6.12g 24%
Sugars: 3.16g
Protein: 31.73g 63%

--Dinner--

Easy Tomato Feta Soup Recipe

Easy Tomato Feta Soup Recipe - Low Calorie, Low Carb, Keto - simple to make with just a few simple, basic ingredients. Creamy tomato soup with basil and rich, savory feta cheese. Ready in 30 minutes on the stove top.

Prep Time:5 mins
Cook Time:25 mins
Total Time:30 mins
Servings: 6

Ingredients

2 tbsp olive oil or butter
¼ cup chopped onion
2 cloves garlic
½ tsp salt
1/8 tsp black pepper
1 tsp pesto sauce — optional
½ tsp dried oregano
1 tsp dried basil
1 tbsp tomato paste — optional
10 tomatoes, skinned, seeded and chopped — or two 14.5 oz cans of peeled tomatoes
1 tsp honey, sugar or erythritol — optional
3 cups water
1/3 cup heavy cream
2/3 cup feta cheese — crumbled

Instructions

Heat olive oil (butter) over medium heat in a large pot (Dutch Oven). Add the onion and cook for 2 minutes, stirring frequently. Add the garlic and cook for 1 minute. Add tomatoes, salt, pepper, pesto (optional), oregano, basil, tomato paste and water. Bring to a boil, then reduce to a simmer. Add sweetener.

Cook on medium heat for 20 minutes, until the tomatoes are tender and cooked. Using an immersion blender, blend until smooth. Add the cream and feta cheese. Cook for 1 more minute.

Add more salt if needed. Serve warm.

Nutrition Info

Calories: 170, Fat: 13g, Saturated Fat: 8g, Cholesterol: 43mg, Sodium: 464mg, Potassium: 542mg, Carbohydrates: 10g, Fiber: 2g, Sugar: 6g, Protein: 4g, Vitamin A: 43%, Vitamin C: 35.7%, Calcium: 11.9%, Iron: 4.9%

Day 5

--Breakfast--

Keto Banana Nut Muffins

Tired of eggs for keto breakfast? These Keto Banana Nut Muffins are so simple and delicious, your kids will love helping you make them on the weekends just as much as they'll love helping you eat them!

Prep Time: 10 Minutes
Cook Time: 20 Minutes
Total Time: 30 minutes
Servings: 10 Muffins

Ingredients

Muffin Battter

> 1 ¼ Cup almond flour (I use this)
> ½ Cup powdered erythritol (I use this)
> 2 tablespoons ground flax (feel free to omit if you don't have it...it just adds a bit more depth to the flavors)
> 2 teaspoons baking powder
> ½ teaspoons ground cinnamon
> 5 tablespoons butter, melted
> 2 ½ teaspoons banana extract
> 1 teaspoon vanilla extract
> ¼ cup unsweetened almond milk
> ¼ cup sour cream

2 eggs

Walnut Crumble

    3/4 cup chopped walnuts
    1 tablespoon butter, cold and cut in 4 pieces
    1 tablespoon almond flour
    1 tablespoon powdered erythritol

Instructions

Preheat oven to 350

Prepare muffin tin with 10 paper liners and set aside.

In a large bowl, mix almond flour, erythritol (or preferred sweetener) flax, baking powder and cinnamon.

Stir in butter, banana extract, vanilla extract, almond milk, and sour cream.

Add eggs to the mixture and gently stir until fully combined.

Fill muffin tins about ½ -3/4 full with mixture.

**If you need more accurate measurements, weigh the batter on a food scale and divide by 10. That will give you the grams of batter per cup.

Crumble Topping

Add walnuts, butter, and almond flour to food processor.

Pulse a few times until nuts are chopped into small pieces. If mixture seems too dry (sometimes some walnuts are softer than others), feel free to add another tablespoon of butter.

Sprinkle bits of the mixture evenly over batter and gently press down.

Sprinkle erythritol on top of crumble mixture.

Bake for 20 minutes or until golden and toothpick comes out clean. Let cool for at least 30 minutes, an hour or more if possible. This lets them firm up.

*If they seem to be cooking faster, take them out sooner to avoid burning. Alternatively, if they are still wet looking, return them to the oven for a few minutes keeping a close eye on them.

--Lunch--

Salmon & Avocado Nori Rolls (Paleo Sushi)

Prep time: 10 mins
Total time: 10 mins
Recipe type: Lunch
Serves: 1

Ingredients

> 3 square nori sheets (seaweed wrappers)
> 150-180 g / 5-6 oz cooked salmon or tinned salmon
> ½ red pepper, sliced into thin strips
> ½ avocado, sliced into strips
> ½ small cucumber, sliced into strips
> 1 spring onion/scallion, cut into 2-3" pieces
> 2 tablespoons mayonnaise
> 1 tablespoon hot sauce or Sriracha sauce
> 1 teaspoon black or white sesame seeds
> Coconut aminos for dipping, optional

Instructions

Place the nori sheet on a flat surface, such as a cutting board, shiny side down. Look at the fibres of the wrapper to see which way it needs to be rolled.

Add a third of the salmon to the right or left third of the nori sheet and top with two strips of pepper, cucumber and avocado. Add some green onion and a drizzle of mayonnaise and hot sauce. You can sprinkle with sesame seeds now or at a later stage, once the rolls are cut.

Lightly wet the top part of the nori sheet (the side you are rolling towards), just 1-2 cm of the wrapper. Pick up the opposite outer edge of the roll and start wrapping it over the ingredients, using your fingers to keep it nice and tight. This can take a bit of practice, but don't worry if your roll doesn't look perfect. Roll it until the top edge of the wrapper overlaps the roll and press it tightly to stick. Place the roll on the cutting board with the seam facing down and then cut into bite-size pieces.

Serve right away with some coconut aminos or extra mayo for dipping, or pack in a container to take for lunch or keep as a snack in the fridge.

--Dinner--

Keto Chicken Pot Pie

Cook Time: 22 mins
Course: Main Course
Servings: 8 servings
Calories: 297kcal

Ingredients

For the Chicken Pot Pie Filling:

> 2 tablespoons of butter
> ½ cup mixed veggies could also substitute green beans or broccoli
> ¼ small onion diced
> ¼ tsp pink salt
> ¼ tsp pepper
> 2 garlic cloves minced
> ¾ cup heavy whipping cream
> 1 cup chicken broth
> 1 tsp poultry seasoning
> ¼ tsp rosemary
> pinch thyme
> 2 ½ cups cooked chicken diced
> ¼ tsp Xanthan Gum

For the crust:

> 4 1/2 tablespoons of butter melted and cooled

1/3 cup coconut flour

2 tablespoons full fat sour cream

4 eggs

¼ teaspoon salt

¼ teaspoon baking powder

1 1/3 cup sharp shredded cheddar cheese or mozzarella shredded

Instructions

Cook 1 to 1 ½ lbs chicken in the slow cooker for 3 hours on high or 6 hours on low.

Preheat oven to 400 degrees.

Sautee onion, mixed veggies, garlic cloves, salt, and pepper in 2 tablespoons butter in an oven safe skillet for approx 5 min or until onions are translucent.

Add heavy whipping cream, chicken broth, poultry seasoning, thyme, and rosemary.

Sprinkle Xanthan Gum on top and simmer for 5 minutes so that the sauce thickens. Make sure to simmer covered as the liquid will evaporate otherwise. You need a lot of liquid for this recipe, otherwise, it will be dry.

Add diced chicken.

Make the breading by combining melted butter (I cool mine by popping the bowl in the fridge for 5 min), eggs, salt, and sour cream in a bowl then whisk together.

Add coconut flour and baking powder to the mixture and stir until combined.

Stir in cheese.

Drop batter by dollops on top of the chicken pot pie. Do not spread it out, as the coconut flour will absorb too much of the liquid.

Bake in a 400-degree oven for 15-20 min.

Set oven to broil and move chicken pot pie to top shelf. Broil for 1-2 minutes until bread topping is nicely browned.

Nutrition Info

Calories: 297kcal
Carbohydrates: 5.3g
Protein: 11.6g
Fat: 17g
Fiber: 2g

Day 6

Avocado Egg Boats

Prep Time: 0 hours 10 mins
Total Time: 0 hours 30 mins

Ingredients

2 ripe avocados, pitted and halved
4 large eggs
kosher salt
Freshly ground black pepper
3 slices bacon
Freshly chopped chives, for garnish

Instructions

Preheat oven to 350°. Place avocados in a baking dish, then crack eggs into a bowl. Using a spoon, transfer yolks to each avocado half, then spoon in as much egg white as you can fit without spilling over.

Season with salt and pepper and bake until whites are set and yolks are no longer runny, about 20 minutes. (Cover with foil if avocados are beginning to brown.)

Meanwhile, in a large skillet over medium heat, cook bacon until crisp, 8 minutes, then transfer to a paper towel-lined plate and chop.

Top avocados with bacon and chives and serve with a spoon.

--Lunch--

Almond Coconut Curry on Veges

This almond coconut curry is super speedy and simple and tastes extraordinary as well! It flaunts nutritious vegetables alongside solid fats and a decent calorie tally.

Total Time: 15 minutes
Servings 4
Calories: 439 kcal

Ingredients

For the veges
For the curry

> 1 tsp coconut oil
> 400 ml coconut milk
> 2 cups mushrooms
> 125g almond butter (100% ground almonds)
> 4 cups spinach
> 1 tbsp tomato paste
> 2 cups brocolli (chopped into florets)
> 1 tbsp curry powder

Instructions

For the curry mixture

Put the coconut drain, almond spread, tomato glue and curry powder in a blender. Mix for around 20 seconds or until smooth.

Add the curry blend to a pan on low-medium warmth and warmth for 10-15 minutes or until warmed through. Blend habitually to abstain from staying.

For the veggies

Heat the coconut oil in a container on medium-high warmth and include the broccoli and mushrooms. Sear for around 3 minutes. Include the spinach and warmth for one more moment.

Serve the veges in a bowl with the curry blend poured over the best.

Recipe Notes:

You can make the almond margarine by granulating almonds in a sustenance processor.

The curry blend isolates whenever it's left to sit in the refrigerator for some time, so make certain to mix it completely before utilizing on the off chance that you have put away it in the ice chest.

Nutrition Info

Calories: 438
Fats: 41g

Protein: 11g
Net Carbs: 9g

--Dinner--

Instant Pot Beef Bourguignon

Instant Pot Beef Bourguignon is a pressure cooker recipe with beef, mushrooms, onions, and carrots cooked in red wine. Low carb, keto, and gluten free.

Prep Time: 30 minutes
Cook Time: 50 minutes
Servings: 6 servings
Calories: 220 kcal

Ingredients

1.5 - 2 pounds beef chuck roast cut into ¾ -inch cubes
5 strips bacon diced
1 small onion chopped
10 ounces cremini mushrooms quartered
2 carrots chopped
5 cloves garlic minced
3 bay leaves
¾ cup dry red wine
¾ teaspoon xanthan gum (or corn starch, read post for instructions)
1 tablespoon tomato paste
1 teaspoon dried thyme
salt & pepper

Instructions

Generously season beef chunks with salt and pepper, and set aside. Select the saute mode on the pressure cooker for medium heat. When the display reads HOT, add diced bacon and cook for about 5 minutes until crispy, stirring fre▢uently. Transfer the bacon to a paper towel lined plate.

Add the beef to the pot in a single layer and cook for a few minutes to brown, then flip and repeat for the other side. Transfer to a plate when done.

Add onions and garlic. Cook for a few minutes to soften, stirring fre▢uently. Add red wine and tomato paste, using a wooden spoon to briefly scrape up flavorful brown bits stuck to the bottom of the pot. Stir to check that the tomato paste is dissolved. Turn off the saute mode.

Transfer the beef back to the pot. Add mushrooms, carrots, and thyme, stirring together. Top with bay leaves. Secure and seal the lid. Cook at high pressure for 40 minutes, followed by a manual pressure release.

Uncover and select the saute mode. Remove bay leaves. Evenly sprinkle xanthan gum over the pot and stir together. Let the stew boil for a minute to thicken while stirring. Turn off the saute mode. Serve into bowls and top with crispy bacon.

Nutrition Info

Calories: 220
Total Fat: 5g 8%

Sodium: 310mg 13%
Potassium: 130mg 4%
Total Carb: 6.5g 2%
Dietary Fiber: 1g 3%
Sugars: 2g
Protein: 27g

Day 7

Keto Cannoli Stuffed Crepes – Low Carb

These Keto Cannoli Stuffed Crepes are perfect for any special occasion breakfast or brunch! Tastes like you're cheating but they are low carb, gluten free, grain free, Atkins and nut free too!

Prep Time: 15 minutes
Cook Time: 20 minutes
Total Time: 35 minutes
Servings: 4 servings

Ingredients

For the crepes:

> 8 ounces cream cheese, softened
> 8 eggs
> ½ teaspoon ground cinnamon
> 1 tablespoon granulated erythritol sweetener
> 2 tablespoons butter, for the pan

For the cannoli filling:

> 6 ounces mascarpone cheese, softened
> 1 cup whole milk ricotta cheese
> ½ teaspoon lemon zest
> ½ teaspoon ground cinnamon

¼ teaspoon unsweetened vanilla extract
¼ cup powdered erythritol sweetener

For the optional chocolate drizzle (not included in nutrition info:)

3 squares of a Lindt 90% chocolate bar

Instructions

For the crepes:

Combine all of the crepes ingredients in a blender and blend until smooth.

Let the batter rest for 5 minutes and then give it a stir to break up any additional air bubbles.

Heat 1 teaspoon of butter in a 10 inch or larger non-stick saute pan over medium heat.

When the butter is melted and bubbling, pour in about ¼ cup of batter (you can eyeball it) and if necessary, gently tilt the pan in a circular motion to create a 6-inch (-ish) round crepe.

Cook for two minutes, or until the top is no longer glossy and bubbles have formed almost to the middle of the crepe.

Carefully flip and cook for another 30 seconds. Remove and place on a plate.

Repeat until you have 8 usable crepes.

Nutrition Info

Serving Size: 2 stuffed crepes
Calories: 478
Fat: 42g
Carbohydrates: 4g
Fiber: 0g
Protein: 16g

--Lunch--

Keto Chicken Enchilada Bowl

This Keto Chicken Enchilada Bowl is a low carb twist on a Mexican favorite!

Prep Time: 20 minutes
Cook Time: 30 minutes
Total Time: 50 minutes
Servings: 4 servings

Ingredients

2 tablespoons coconut oil (for searing chicken)
1 pound of boneless, skinless chicken thighs
¾ cup red enchilada sauce (recipe from Low Carb Maven)
¼ cup water
¼ cup chopped onion
4 oz can diced green chiles

Toppings (feel free to customize)

1 whole avocado, diced
1 cup shredded cheese (I used mild cheddar)
¼ cup chopped pickled jalapenos
½ cup sour cream
1 roma tomato, chopped

CPSIA information can be obtained
at www.ICGtesting.com
Printed in the USA
FSHW022122170520
70328FS